THE COLORING BOOK
A Carry Along Companion

Illustrations By
Christopher Cuyler

Contact: WWW.CUYLERART.COM

TEST PAGE

WELCOME

Please use this page to test any drawing materials you may be considering.

*I highly recommend putting 1 or 2 peices of paper between each design if you use marker.

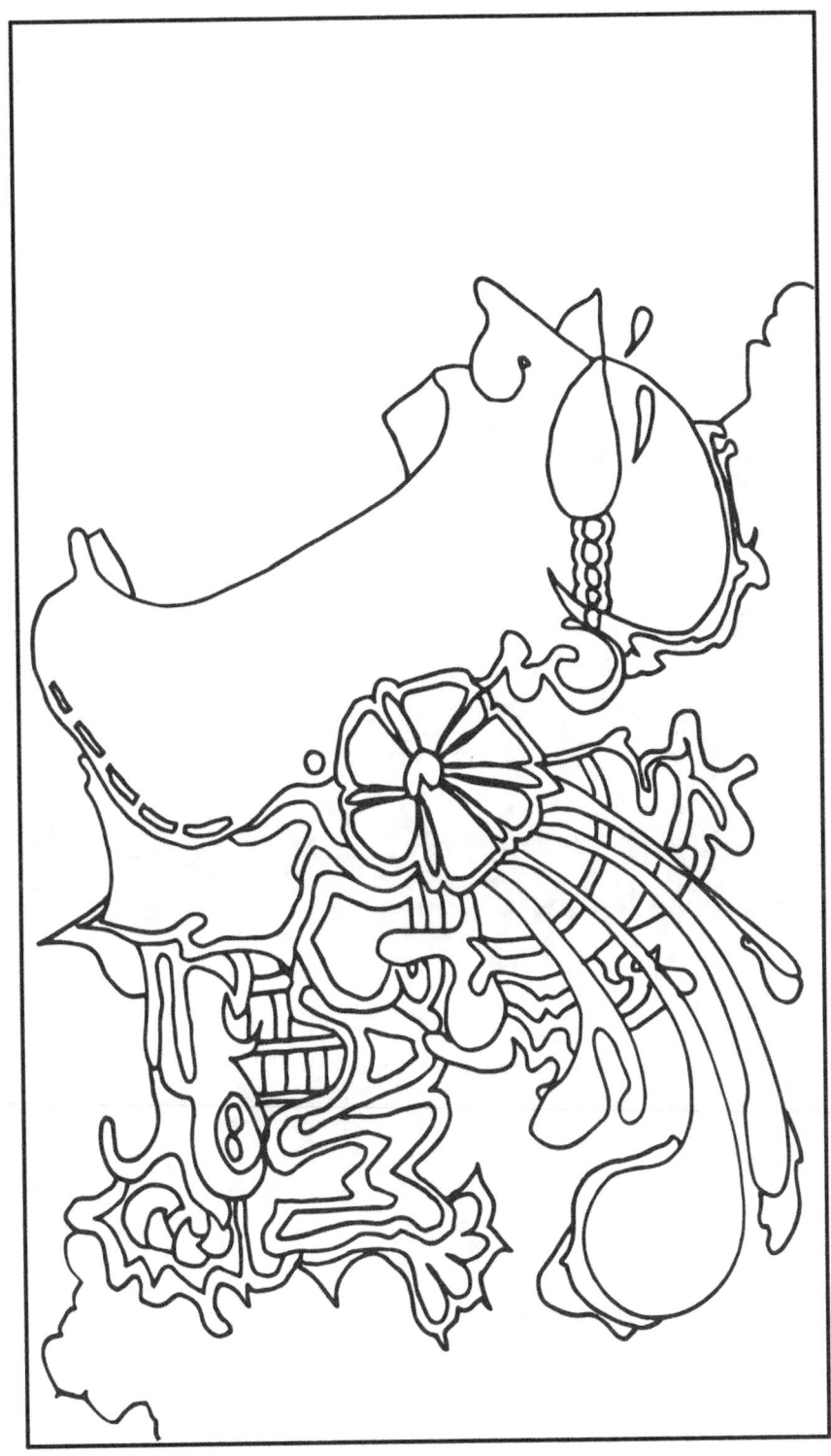

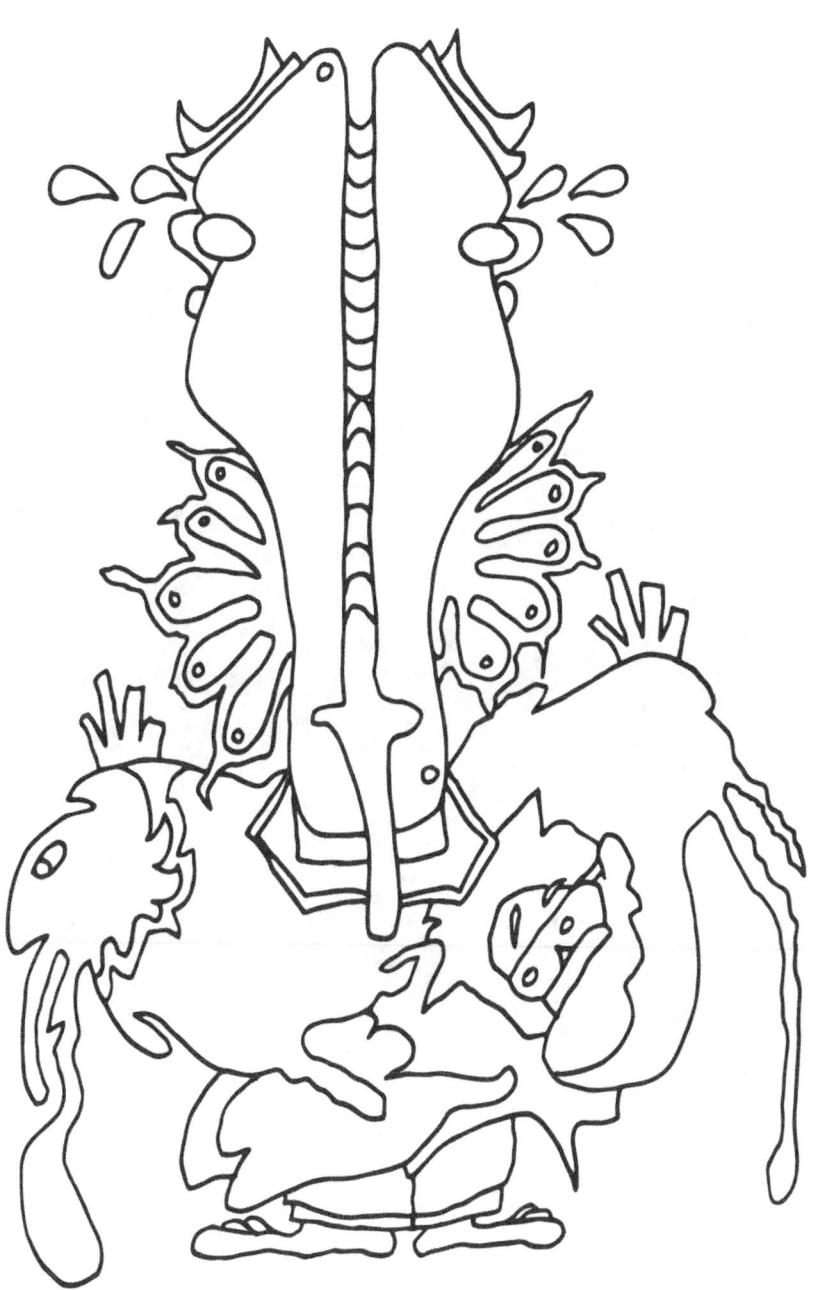

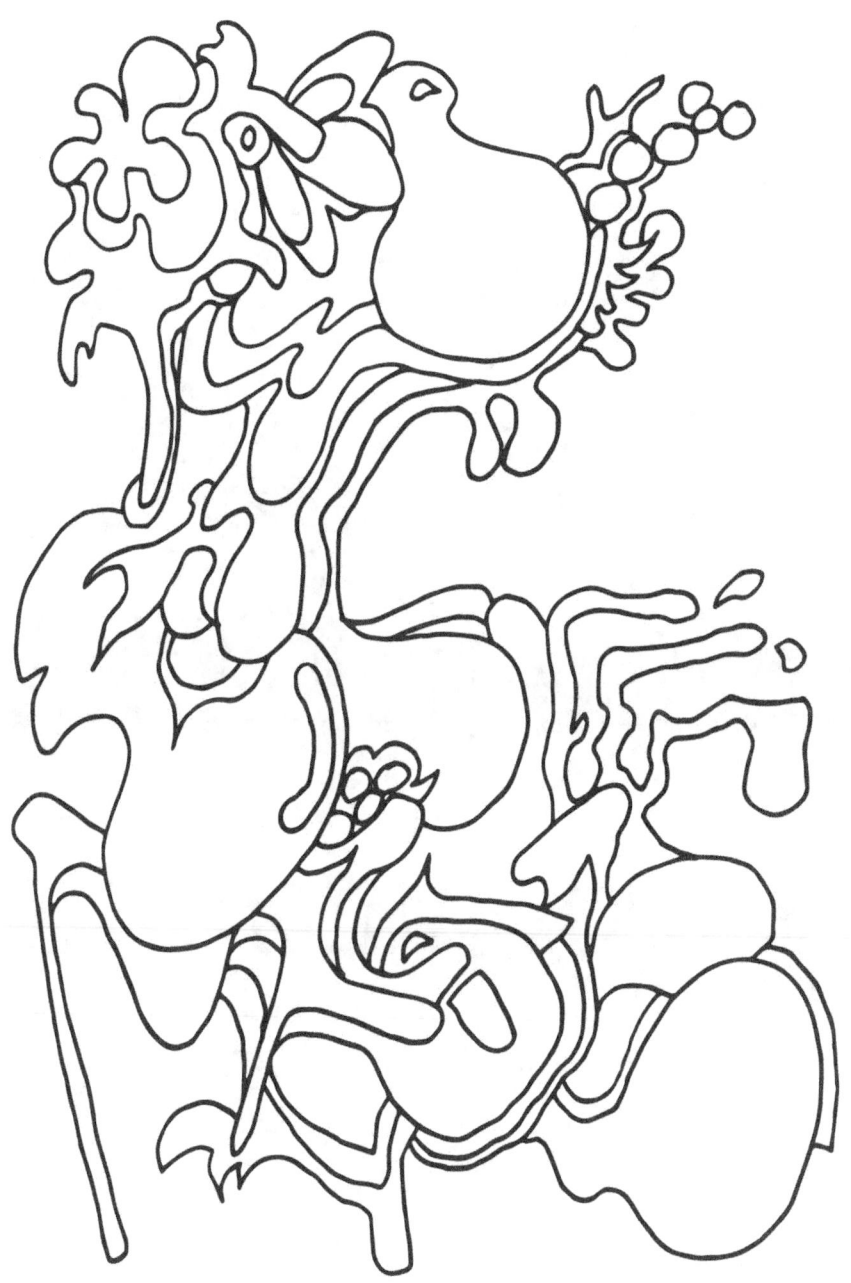

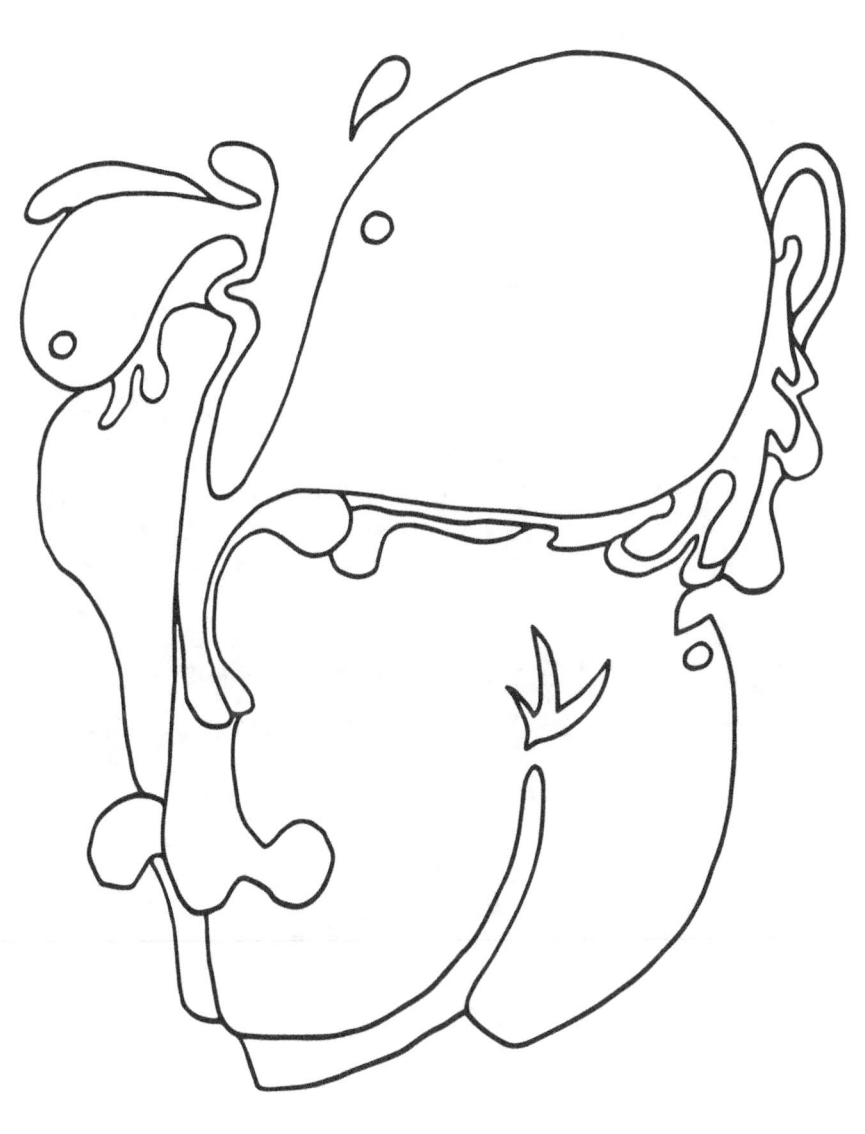

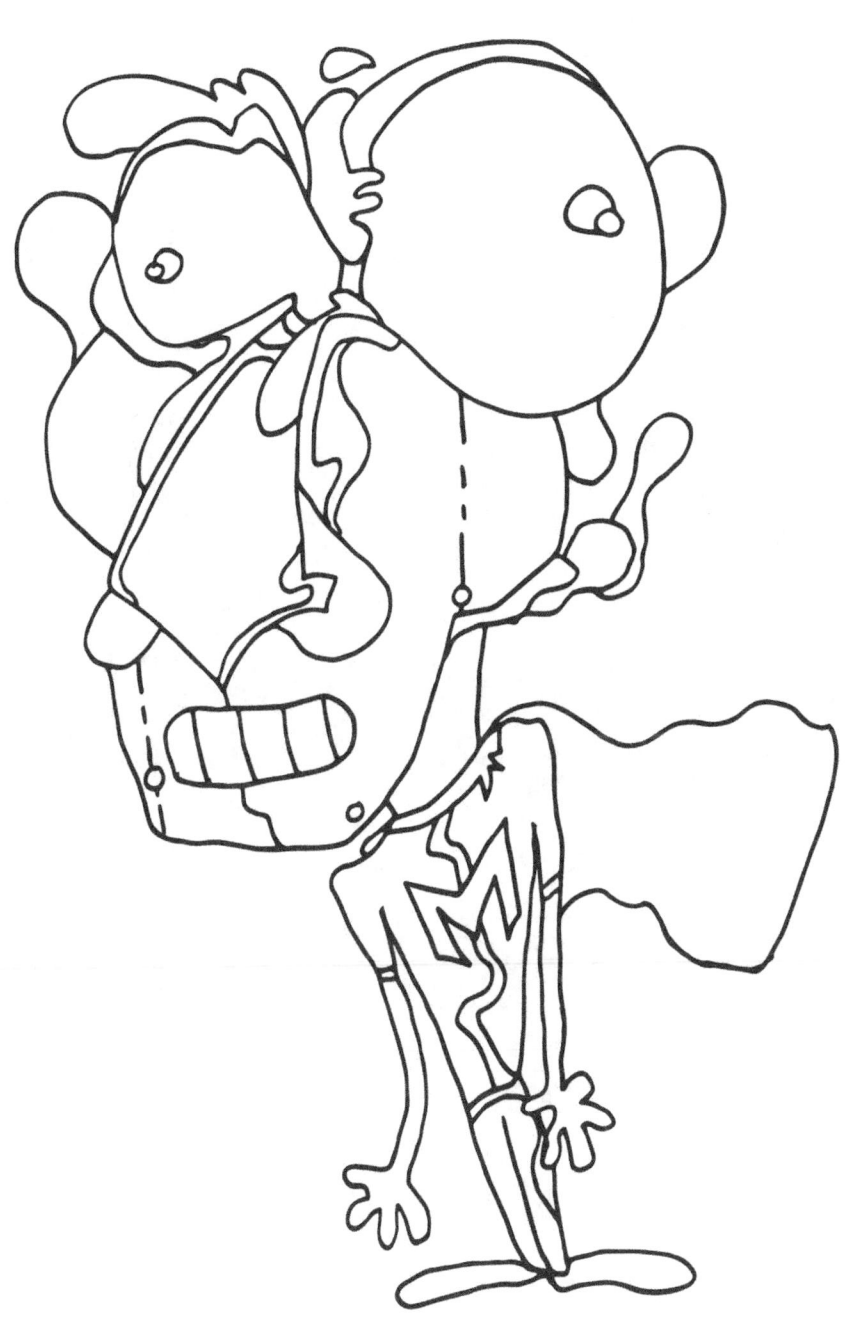

www.ingramcontent.com/pod-product-compliance
Lightning Source LLC
Chambersburg PA
CBHW062118280526
45788CB00003B/1507